2-07

THE SECRETS OF SUCCESSFUL BUYING AND SELLING ON eBay

ROGER SHAW

DISCARD

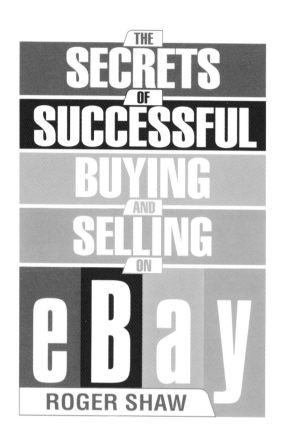

THE SECRETS OF SUCCESSFUL BUYING AND SELLING ON eBay

ROGER SHAW

foulsham

LONDON • NEW YORK • TORONTO • SYDNEY

Dedication

In memory of Daniel Shaw

Acknowledgements

I would like to thank my lovely wife Gail for her love, support and understanding during the writing of this book, and our children, Ashley, Bethany, Jonathan and Paige, whose need for the latest games, gadgets and toys first grew my interest in eBay all those years ago.

Finally, my mother, Violet Shaw, for her encouragement and love throughout my life.

foulsham

The Publishing House, Bennetts Close, Cippenham, Slough, Berkshire, SL1 5AP, England

Foulsham books can be found in all good bookshops and direct from www.foulsham.com

ISBN-13: 978-0-572-03096-4
ISBN-10: 0-572-03096-7

A CIP record for this book is available from the British Library

Printed in China through Colorcraft Ltd.,HK

Contents

Introduction

There can't be anyone who hasn't at least heard about eBay. It is a modern phenomenon, one of the fastest-growing businesses in the world, with an astonishing client base.

You may already have tried buying or selling on eBay. You may have taken a look and found it all a bit intimidating. Some of you will have simply heard about this huge internet auction site through a friend, or perhaps through its advertising. But whatever your experience of eBay, your age or your interests, and whether you want to buy, sell or both, this step-by step guide will soon have you buying and selling like an expert.

Like many of the world's largest companies and corporations, eBay has its roots in the most humble beginnings. In September 1995, Pierre Omidyar started eBay in his living room with an idea to create

a community where individuals and merchants have equal opportunity to buy and sell new and used goods at fair prices – or in other words for his fiancée Pam to buy and meet collectors of the Pez™ sweet candy dispensers!

eBay has come a long way since then, with well over 100 million registered users buying and selling everything from Concorde parts and antiques to classic cars and the latest gadgets. The most expensive item sold so far was a jet for £2.8 million!

The eBay website may at first glance appear complex, but don't let this put you off. It has been very well designed so it is really quite easy to use. It is also very sophisticated, with multi-layered elements and options. This book is not a complete works because that would make for a huge tome! I've aimed to make the whole process accessible and easy to understand and use. I've left out a lot of information in order to bring you a uniquely simple guide that's packed full with tips and secrets. Step-by-step instructions, together with real eBay screen shots, will take you through the process of registering, buying and selling. You'll soon discover the short cuts to success, as well as how to avoid the pitfalls. This practical guide will give you knowledge to pick up the bargains and achieve the highest price for items you wish to sell on eBay.

CHAPTER 1

Finding Your Way Around

This chapter will introduce you to the basics of eBay so you can get registered and begin to find your way around.

How eBay works

Quite simply, eBay brings buyers and sellers together via its website. All sellers pay a listing fee and a commission to eBay when an item is sold. eBay makes no charge to buyers.

The online auction

An auction room works with a hall full of customers bidding on an entered lot; eBay works in just the same way but via the internet, thus creating a virtual hall where many millions of people can enter and bid.

If you want to buy, you simply turn up and bid. If you want to sell, there are various ways of making your item as attractive as possible: using good descriptions, photographs, listing for between one and ten days, and so on. All items on eBay display the time and date when the auction will finish and buyers can place a bid at any time before the item ends. In addition, some have a 'Buy it now price', which means you can purchase the item immediately for the price shown.

The object of this book is to show you step by step how to buy, how to sell, and how to get the best out of eBay.

Getting started

This couldn't be easier! Type **www.ebay.co.uk** into your web browser and it will take you to the UK website. If you live outside the UK, then type in eBay's web address for your country. For example, you would type **www.ebay.com** for the US.

The eBay home page

This will open eBay's home page. Since it changes all the time, it won't look exactly like the pages shown here, but it will look very similar. It will change again once you are registered. The key elements are always shown at the top menu on the home page, including 'Search', 'My eBay', 'Buy' and 'Sell'.

Registering — becoming an eBay member

To buy or sell on eBay you must first become a member. It's quick and easy and is done via the eBay website.

The first step is to open eBay's home page in your web browser by typing **www.ebay.co.uk** for the UK or **www.ebay.com** for the US. Your computer will open the current eBay home page. Obviously eBay updates its site all the time, so you'll see something similar to this screen.

Click on the **Register** button. This link will take you through the registration form.

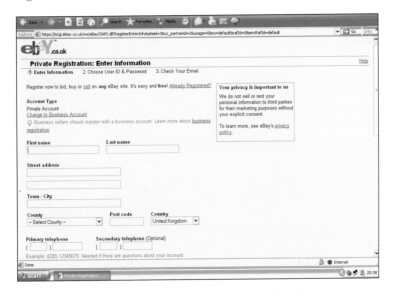

Fill out your name, address and contact details by clicking on each box in turn. Don't worry if you make a mistake. Any errors or missing information will be highlighted in red and you will be asked to fill out the box again.

Your e-mail address

Your e-mail address is how eBay, sellers and buyers will contact you. It is important that you use an address you have regular access to. Most e-mail accounts allow you to access them from any computer, which can be useful for keeping an eye on your accounts while at work, on holiday or away from home.

If you want to set up an e-mail address just for eBay use, you can do so free of charge at many websites, the most popular being www.msn.com and www.yahoo.com. However, if you use either of these you will be asked for your credit or debit card information. Don't worry: you will never be charged without your consent and your card information is kept strictly confidential. This process of providing eBay with your card information helps it to confirm who you are for its security purposes.

User agreement and privacy policy

During the registration process, you will find a link to details of eBay's terms and conditions. You should read them to ensure you are happy with them, then click on the three boxes confirming that you have read them and that you are 18 years of age or over.

Choosing your user ID

Everyone chooses a user ID, the name by which they are known on eBay, and a password so that only they can have access to their eBay information.

As your user ID is how other members identify you, you should spend a little time choosing something suitable. Try to think of an ID that is easy to remember, not too complicated, and perhaps describes your interests. It is best to avoid obscene or silly names; they might seem funny at the time and appeal to you, but many members might be put off when buying from the 'killerkid' or 'dodgydan'!

To make choosing a user ID easier, eBay will suggest a few user IDs, usually linked around your name. If you are happy with one of these, click next to it. Otherwise, fill in the name you want. Once you are happy with the name, click on **Create your own ID**.

You can change your user ID at any time, although if you do this, a 'Changed ID' icon is shown next to your ID. This can deter buyers and sellers if they suspect this may be an attempt to hide your eBay past.

User ID already taken

With the many millions of eBay members, there is a good chance your first choice of user ID may already be in use. If this happens, eBay will guide you through choosing a different ID and will even offer you some suggestions.

Your eBay password

Your eBay password is the only means you have of preventing others from having access to your eBay account. When signing into your account, you will be asked for your user ID and your password. It is really important you tell no one of your password and make sure you change it regularly.

Security tip

Choose your password carefully, using the advice below. Don't write it down or share it with anyone, and change it regularly.

I recommend that your password should:

• Be six to eight characters long;

• Be made up of a mixture of capital letters, numbers and special characters;

• Not include words that can be found in a dictionary;

• Be impossible to guess.

If you submit a poor password – your name, for example – eBay will reject it and ask you for another.

Security meter

To help you with password security, eBay has come up with a security meter. As you type in your chosen password, a bar appears; the darker the bar, the more secure the password.

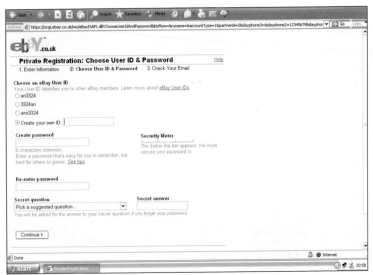

Secret question

If you ever forget you password, eBay will ask you to confirm your answer to your selected secret question before sending your password to you by e-mail. It provides a list of options for you to choose from: for example, 'What street did you grow up on?' or 'What is your mother's maiden name?' You must select a question and type in your answer, making sure it's a reply that's easy to remember.

Finalising your registration

You will be pleased to know that you are almost there with regards to registering an eBay account and becoming a member.

Confirm your identity

eBay needs assurance that you are who you say you are.

If you have used a Hotmail or a Yahoo e-mail address, you will be asked to confirm your identity by providing debit or credit card details. Don't worry: you will not be charged and your card details are kept very safe within eBay.

If you have used an e-mail address offered by an internet service provider such as AOL or Wannado, then you are not required to enter your credit card details.

Check your e-mail

You will then be taken to the 'Check Your E-mail' web page, either direct from the previous page if you are with a standard ISP, or once your card details have been accepted if you are with Yahoo or a similar provider.

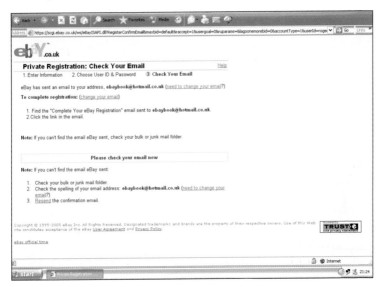

Open the e-mail account you have provided eBay and look for the e-mail it has just sent you. If nothing appears in your inbox, check your junk mail folders, as some ISPs or spam filters will reject this kind of e-mail. If so, identify the sender as 'Not spam' and retrieve the e-mail.

Security tip

Never click again on any other links in e-mails, even if they appear to be from eBay. This is the only time you need to. Fake e-mails are circulated in which you are asked to confirm your name, password and/or credit card details. They will look authentic; they are not.

Once you have opened the e-mail, click on the link. This will confirm your registration.

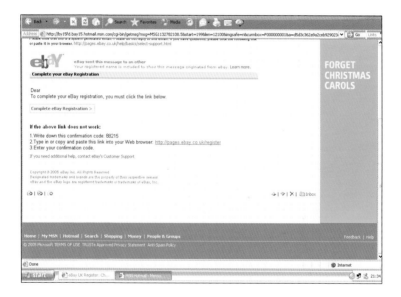

Signing in and out

That's it! Now you are an eBay member. Each time you visit the site, you will be asked to sign in, using your user ID and password.

To sign in, go to the eBay home page and click on **Sign in** at the top of the page.

You will then be asked for your eBay user ID and password. Fill out the boxes by clicking on each one in turn, then click on **Sign in**.

You can then go wherever you like on the site, using the menus and links provided.

When you have finished visiting eBay, always sign out to prevent anyone else from using your account. This is especially important if you have visited eBay from your work station or an internet café.

From the home page, simply click on **Sign out**. When you have successfully signed out from your account, you will see a message to confirm this.

My eBay

Each time you sign in to your account, you will be taken to the eBay home page. It will look slightly different every time you visit because it is constantly updated, but the top menu will remain roughly the same. You should see the message 'Welcome to eBay', then your username.

Now click on **My eBay**. This is one of eBay's most useful features and where you should spend some time exploring because it contains all the information connected with your account: items you are bidding on, things you have bought and sold, feedback, messages and so on.

My eBay site map flowchart

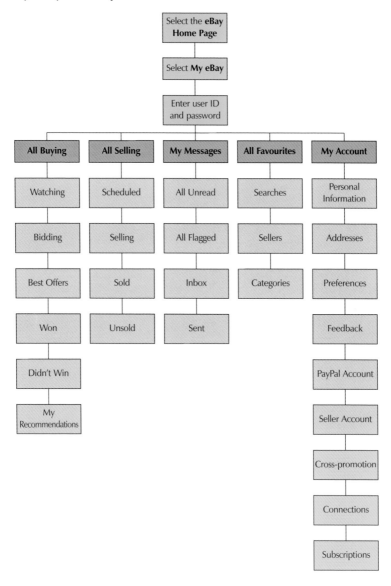

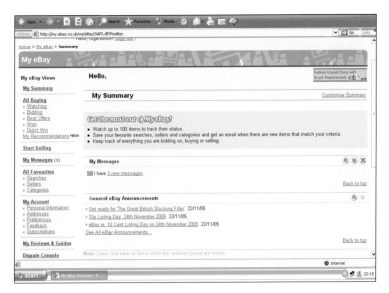

'My eBay' is full of so much information, it may seem a little complicated at first glance, but if you take it step by step, investigating sections as you need to use them, you'll soon find your way around.

'My Summary' section shows your recent account activity, listing the details of any items you are buying or selling. To start with, this is the most useful section. It will show you the details of the item, whether you are the highest bidder, how long before the auction ends, and other useful information. This section also includes 'Items I'm Watching'. If you don't want to bid on an item but would like to keep an eye on how the auction progresses, you can add it to this list.

On the left side of the screen you will see a list of links associated with your eBay account. Here are just a few:

All buying

• **Watching:** Lists the items within your watch list.

• **Bidding:** Displays items you are bidding on.

• **Best offers:** Shows items that you have made a best offer on.

• **Won:** Lists 'Buy It Now' items and items you have won at auction.

- **Didn't win:** Lists items you did not win.

- **My recommendations:** Lists your recommended sellers.

All selling
- **Scheduled:** Shows items you have scheduled for sale.

- **Selling:** Displays items you are selling.

- **Sold:** Lists items you have sold.

- **Unsold:** Shows the items that you did not sell.

My messages
Displays your messages from eBay. In most cases you will also be sent a copy via your e-mail address.

All favourites
- **Searches:** A useful feature that lists your favourite searches.

- **Sellers:** Shows your favourite sellers.

- **Categories:** Lists your favourite categories.

This has just given you the basics and scratched the surface of 'My eBay', so when you have some spare time, look and click on the many links and discover for yourself what they all do.

Search tips

With the millions of items offered on eBay, you might believe finding what you are looking for may take you hours, if not days. Not so. eBay's search tools are really powerful and will take you to what you are looking for in seconds (or slightly longer if you are not on broadband!). If you have ever entered text within one of the many internet search sites, you will find that eBay's search box works in just the same way.

Here are some useful search tips for you to use when you are looking for items offered for sale.

The simplest way is to use eBay's search box. This can be found on eBay's home page and within 'My eBay'. As an example, enter **piano** into the search box.

eBay secrets tip

Some of the best bargains I've found are the ones that have been misspelled by the seller – so other people haven't found them on their searches and there have been fewer – or no – bids! Searching for items under one word or two will also make a difference to the results: for example, you'll get a different set of results if you search for 'Bladerunner' than if you search for 'Blade Runner'.

At the time of writing this book, 'piano' produced over 3,500 items offered for sale.

If you had plenty of time to kill, you could look at each individual item – good luck!

Let's assume that we can be more specific in our requirements and say we are looking for an electric piano. Type **electric piano** in the search box. At the time of writing, 'electric piano' produced only 18 items, a much more manageable number!

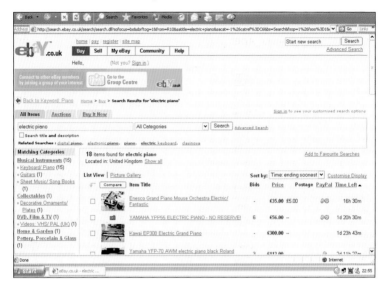

You can also narrow the results by searching for a particular item within a specific category; for example, type **piano** in the search box, then use the drop-down categories menu to search only within musical instruments. The only downside of this option is that not all sellers will list their items in the appropriate categories, or you may be looking for an item that could cross into a few categories.

For rare items, tick the 'In titles and description' option, or click on the advanced search link and fill in the boxes with more details.

Always try to be specific in the keywords you use for your search, and think about other words that sellers may use to describe their items.

There are so many ways to search for items and we have only looked here at the most simple and effective. As you become more experienced, you will soon discover the best way of using and combining keywords to find the items you are looking for.

Saving your favourite searches

Once you have found a way of searching using keywords, categories and so on, eBay will remember it for you and will even send you an e-mail when new items are offered in your favourite categories.

First, enter your favourite search information, then click on **Search**. On the top left-hand corner of the results page, click on the link **Add to favourite searches**.

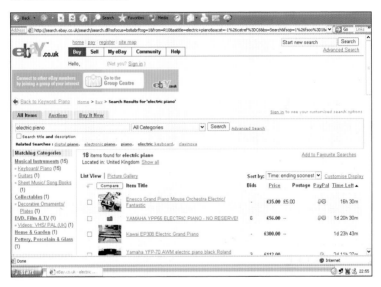

If you have not already done so, you will be asked to sign in to your account. On the 'Favourite searches' page you will see an e-mail tick box. If you don't want an e-mail informing you of new items offered that match your search criteria, then untick the box.

Your favourite searches can be viewed at any time and can be found in 'My eBay'.

Payments

Once you are familiar with the structure of eBay, you'll want to have a go at buying or selling. In this chapter, we'll outline the payment options, and show you how to set up a PayPal account, which is the easiest and most secure way to buy and sell on eBay.

Payment methods

Following a purchase or a sale on eBay, you will have to deal with either sending or receiving a payment. There are a number of payment methods that can be used, depending on the requirements of the seller or buyer. When you pay for an item, the seller will usually indicate a preferred payment method, and you can indicate your preferred method if you are selling.

By far the safest and quickest method is to use PayPal, eBay's own secure money-transfer system. This allows you to send and receive money swiftly and securely, nationally and internationally.

Cash

Cash is one of the oldest methods of payment and I've used it for collecting goods in person. However, I would never recommend sending cash, even small amounts, by post (even though most sellers would accept it, providing it is sent at the buyer's own risk). It is simply not safe or reliable and is impossible to track.

Security tip

It's a basic but important reminder that you should never send cash through the post. You cannot guarantee that it will arrive, and there is only your word that you sent the right amount and the recipient's word that it did or did not arrive. Don't risk it.

Cheques and postal orders

For UK transactions, cheques and postal orders are easy and relatively safe. The only disadvantage of a cheque is that most sellers will not send items out until your cheque has cleared, so you will have to wait a few days for your purchase.

Bank transfer

A bank transfer moves funds directly to or from your bank account. I am never happy to give out my bank details and would never use this method for high-value items or international purchases.

Money orders

Money orders are available from most banks. Used internationally, they are converted into the local currency in cash by the recipient, so you must therefore treat them in the same way as cash.

Security tip

Criminals use money orders because they are hard to track and give instant cash. Beware of sellers who insist on being paid in this way.

PayPal

As I said at the outset, PayPal is my payment method of preference, and that of most buyers and sellers on eBay.

PayPal is a quick and easy electronic method of payment. It was established in 1999 and has been a huge success. It was so successful, in fact, that eBay purchased the business and since then it has gone from strength to strength.

PayPal allows you to send and collect money electronically using debit and credit cards, your bank account or the funds you have acquired through your own sales. It's now very popular, with more than 78 million account-holding members worldwide. Many eBay members insist on it, allowing them to take instant payments from a possible 45 countries in six currencies.

PayPal also provides a secure way of paying for items using your credit or debit card without the seller knowing your card details, which is ideal for home and international purchases. The highest SSL 128-bit encryption technology is used to keep your details secure and confidential at all times. There is also a buyer and seller protection offered through PayPal that covers you for up to £500.

 Security tip
I would recommend you use a credit card, if you have one, and link it to your PayPal account. Use this card for your purchases as this provides additional protection.

All credit card companies offer a better level of protection than PayPal, so if your goods don't arrive you can make a claim with your credit card company. This is known as a Chargeback. The card company will refund the transaction and recover the money from PayPal.

Registering for a PayPal account

Signing up for PayPal is easy and free. Just follow the links on eBay's home page or type **www.paypal.co.uk** into your web browser. Either route will lead you to PayPal's home page.

Click on the **Sign In** box. You will be offered the choice of a number of different accounts, but we are only really interested in the following two accounts.

PayPal personal account: If you are not interested in selling and are just going to purchase items from eBay, select this account. You can upgrade to a premier account at any time if you change your mind.

PayPal premier account: Many of the current eBay members have a premier PayPal account. This type of account is for both buyers and sellers and gives you the flexibility to be able to receive debit and credit card payments for items you offer for sale on eBay, as well as being able to pay for the items you have bought.

Select the account you require, then select the county or region where you live, then click on **Continue**.

You now must complete the account form in a similar way to the eBay form by filling in all the boxes. I would use the same e-mail address you used to register on eBay and perhaps use a different password, but following the same advice as given on page 17. Please make sure your telephone number is correct. PayPal will check this detail later.

There are some additions to the user agreement that you must agree to by ticking **Yes**. To prevent automated registrations, the additional security measure of a random text box has been introduced. Simply type the characters that appear into the blank box on the right, then click on **Sign up**.

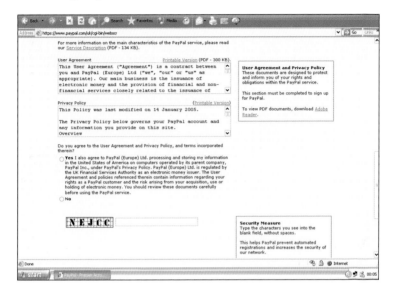

Confirming your PayPal registration

In a similar way to the eBay registration, PayPal will send you an e-mail with a link button asking you to activate your account.

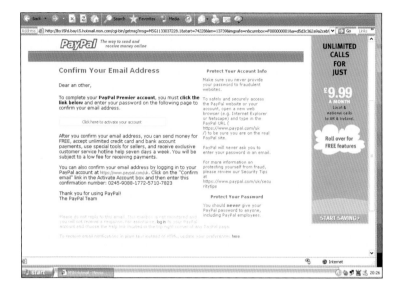

Click on the link, enter your password and your PayPal account is up and running.

Once you have opened your account, you may decide you don't need to send payments by any other route!

Your PayPal account

Once you have registered with PayPal, you can choose to pay for goods through your PayPal account.

If have been a successful seller, you will soon build up a balance of cash within this account. Use this balance for paying your eBay fees, and transfer amounts of £50 or more to your bank account to avoid transaction fees. Don't keep lots of money in your PayPal account as no interest is paid on the account.

PayPal fees

Little in life is free. PayPal offers a great service but charges a small commission. Just like eBay, it is the seller who pays the fees. Here is a brief summary of PayPal charges. These will alter from time to time so you should always check the most up-to-date charges for yourself at the time of transaction.

• **To receive funds up to £1,500:** 3.4% of the total amount plus £0.20.

• **To receive funds from £1,500 to £6,000:** 2.9% of the total amount plus £0.20.

• **To transfer funds from your PayPal account to your bank account:** For amounts less than £49.99, the charge is £0.25; for £50.00 and over, there is no charge, but be prepared to wait at least five days for the funds to be credited.

Using your PayPal account

Each time you visit PayPal and log in to your account, this page is displayed, together with an account overview showing your recent activity. On the top of the page you will see a number of tabs linking you to the services available. We will explore the more useful of these services throughout this chapter.

Funding your transactions

Each month, many millions of pounds' worth of transactions are handled by PayPal. To prevent fraud, PayPal has introduced a number of checks to confirm your identity and your address.

All new accounts have a spending limit of £500. If you are a seller, there is no limit to money you can receive into your PayPal account. However, there is a withdrawal limit of £500 per month for a period of three months.

If you wish to send money or purchase items and pay for them via PayPal, you must now register a credit or debit card to fund your transactions. This can be added during the verification process.

The verification process

You will be asked from time to time to verify your account. Once verified, your spending limit will be lifted. The only limit you then have is the balance on your chosen method of payment: your debit or credit card.

To go through the verification process, access your PayPal account by going to its website at www.paypal.co.uk and signing in. Select the **Get Verified** link.

Add your bank account

There are three steps you must complete for your account to be verified.

• Select **Set up bank funding**.

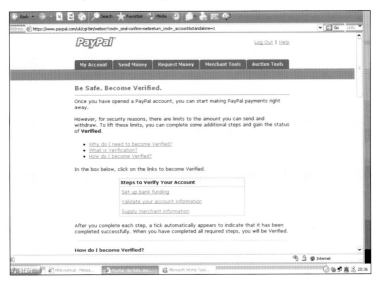

• Choose your country from the drop-down list and click continue.

• You must now fill in all the boxes and reconfirm your banking details. Once you have completed this, select **Add bank account**.

- PayPal will credit two small amounts into your bank account. This usually takes between three and five days. When you see your next bank statement, make a note of these amounts; they will be needed later.

Confirm your bank account and set up a direct debit
- Now access your PayPal account and sign in.

- Next fill in the two boxes with the two small amounts that were credited to your account. This will verify your bank account and you will have completed the first of PayPal's three security checks.

Add your credit or debit card and validate your account information
- The next step is to add your credit or debit card details. Once logged in to your PayPal account, select the **Get Verified** link.

- If you have been successful in setting up and validating your direct debit, a tick will appear in the first box confirming that the first of the three steps has been completed.

• Now select **Validate your account information**. Take your time to fill in all the boxes with your credit or debit card information.

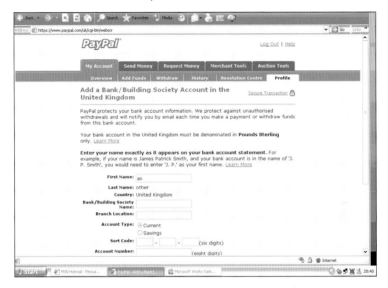

Security tip

PayPal's three-stage verification process may seem a nuisance, but it does offer you a high level of security on your internet transactions, so it is well worth it.

Once you have completed the boxes, select the **Add card** button at the bottom of the page.

Validate your account information by phone

* In the next step, PayPal will ask you to check that the address and home telephone number you registered with your debit or credit card are correct.

To help combat fraud and protect its members, PayPal makes an automated phone call to the telephone number entered for your address, so please ensure the details you have entered are accurate. You need to have a touch-tone telephone, that is, one on which you hear tones when the buttons are pressed.

At the bottom of the page, you can choose to receive the automated call immediately or in one minute by selecting the appropriate button. Before you click on the **Continue** link, make sure that no one is using the telephone and that you have the phone within reach.

• Once you have clicked **Continue**, PayPal will issue you with a PIN.

• You will shortly receive an automated call from PayPal. When you answer this call, you will be asked for the PIN displayed.

- After you have entered this PIN using the telephone keypad, you can simply hang up.

Congratulations! You have successfully validated your account information and completed stage two of the verification process.

Edit business information

- Once again, you need to be logged in to your PayPal account and to select the **Get Verified** link.

- If you have been successful in validating your account details by phone, a second tick will appear in box two, confirming that this second stage has been completed.

- Now select **Edit business information**.

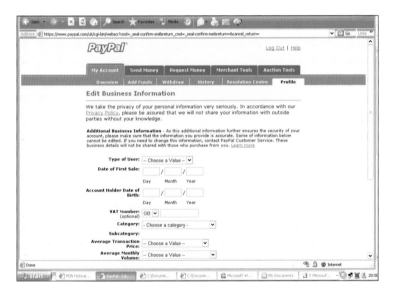

- You will be presented with the final form to complete. It is simple, so try to answer all the questions as best you can. It's there because PayPal has a legal requirement to know a little about you.

- When you have finished, select **Save** and you will have completed the verification process.

Adding funds

There are really only two ways in which money is transferred into your PayPal account. One is from a sale, in which case a buyer will send you money via the PayPal system. The second is that you transfer money yourself from your registered bank account.

Funds from a buyer

When a buyer sends you money via the PayPal system, you will receive an automated e-mail stating, 'You've got new funds!' Within the e-mail will be the amount and who has sent it. There is also a link that will show you the transaction details.

Funds from your bank account

You may at times want to transfer funds from your bank account into your PayPal account. It's a simple process and is free, although do remember that no interest is paid on your PayPal balance and the process usually takes seven to nine working days.

First log in to your PayPal account, then select the **Add funds** option.

eBay secrets tip

It's a good idea to check the amount before requesting a transfer into your PayPal account, and always make sure you have the funds within your bank account to cover the amount.

Now select **Transfer funds from a bank account**, then follow the straightforward instructions.

Transferring funds

If you become a successful seller you will soon build up a balance of cash in your PayPal account. Before you start to transfer it into your bank account, use this balance for paying your eBay fees and for eBay purchases.

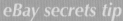

eBay secrets tip

Always try to transfer amounts of £50 or more from PayPal to your bank account to avoid transaction fees. Don't keep lots of money in your PayPal account as no interest is paid.

• First log in to your PayPal account, then select **Withdraw**.

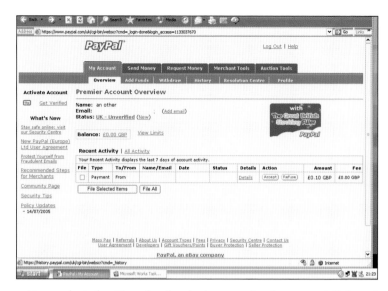

- Now select the **Transfer funds to your bank account** link and follow the straightforward instructions. It will take between five and seven working days for the funds to appear in your bank account.

Paying for goods

There are a number of ways to pay for items that have been won – as outlined in Payment methods on page 33 – and these options are set by the seller. If you are sending a cheque, you will be told the address to send the cheque to.

Paying with PayPal

If you have set up and activated your PayPal account and the seller accepts PayPal – and most do – this is the simplest and most secure option to choose.

Don't worry if there is not enough money in your PayPal account as the payment can be made with a debit or credit card or from your bank account.

Once you have won an item you will be sent a 'Congratulations' e-mail giving details of the item you have won and payment options accepted by the seller.

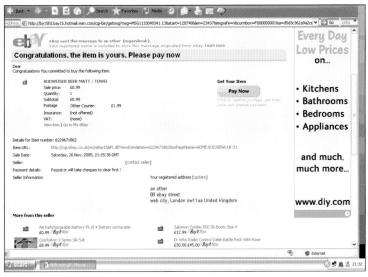

- Select the PayPal link within the e-mail as your payment method, and check all the details are correct. You will be asked to log in to your account to confirm who you are, then click on **Continue**.

Security tip
You may prefer to deal only with eBayers who use PayPal, as an added security protection.

- Next, review all the payment details to ensure that you are happy with your funding options, then click on **Continue**. That's it! Congratulations! You have made your first payment! An e-mail will then be sent to you confirming that a payment has been made.

Being paid for goods

As a seller, you can choose your preferred payment options (see page 33).

Being paid by cheque
Some buyers like to pay by cheque. If you have agreed to accept cheques, then do not send the item until you have received the cheque, paid it into your account, and confirmed that it has cleared and the funds are in you bank.

Being paid by PayPal
If you have selected PayPal as a method of payment, there is not much you have to do as the process is fully automated. Once a buyer pays for your item using PayPal, you will receive an e-mail entitled 'You've got new funds!'

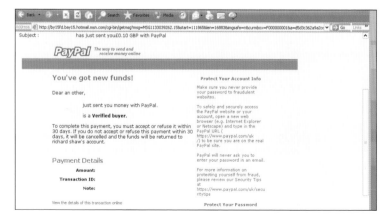

- Log in to your PayPal account, then click on the **History** link to review details of the payment you have received.

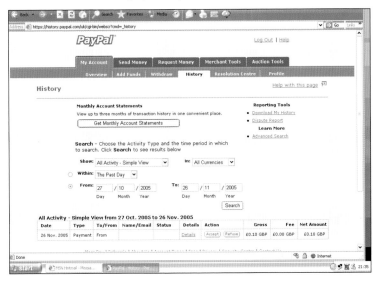

Sending money

There might be occasions where you would like to send money for non-auction goods and this can be done via PayPal.

> **eBay secrets tip**
> You can even use PayPal to send money to a friend for their birthday, for example – particularly useful for overseas relatives or friends.

- Once logged in to your PayPal account, select the **Send money** option.

- Fill out the boxes, including the recipient's e-mail address, then select **Continue**.

- Make sure the payment details are correct. If you wish to change your funding options, select the **More funding options** link found in the 'Source of funds' section.

- When you are happy that everything is correct, click on **Send money** and you're done!

Requesting money

- To request money via PayPal, log in to your PayPal account and select the **Request money** link.

- Fill out the boxes, including the e-mail address of the person who is sending the money, then select **Continue**.

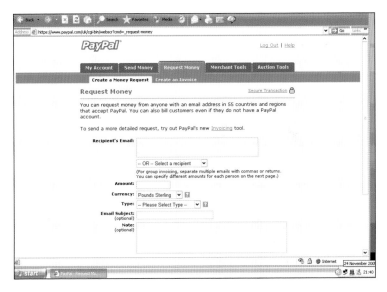

- If you would like to request money and send a detailed invoice, select the **Create an invoice** tab and fill out the boxes.

- When you have completed this page, click **Continue**.

- Next, check all the details, then click **Request money**.

- To check the progress of a money request, log in to your PayPal account, then select the **History** tab and you will see a record of the current position.

Resolving payment disputes

Mistakes do happen, so if you ever have a problem with a purchase or a sale, contact the seller or buyer first. You can do this from the drop-down menu next to the item on 'My eBay'. Remember: co-operation is better than confrontation. Only when you have done this and you find yourself making no progress should you use PayPal's resolution centre.

- Log in to your PayPal account, then select the **Resolution centre** tab.

- Then you simply follow the straightforward procedure to log your claim. You will receive an e-mail acknowledging your dispute information, followed by e-mails to let you know what has been done and how the dispute has been resolved.

Security tip

If you purchased something using a credit card, you may also contact your card issuer as it can offer you additional protection to recover the money.

CHAPTER 3

Guarding Against Fraud

In this chapter

- ❂ How to protect your account
- ❂ Fake e-mails
- ❂ Imaginary items
- ❂ The long fraud
- ❂ Postage scam
- ❂ Protection against viruses

The vast majority of people who use eBay are honest. Sadly, within any community, there are thieves, robbers, burglars, shoplifters, pickpockets, crooks, con artists, fraudsters and people that I could only describe within this book as not being very nice. They are all on eBay, together with all the many very honest people, like you and me! You can – and should – take some simple steps to ensure that you don't fall victim to such people. eBay itself works tirelessly to try to prevent fraudulent activity on its site.

How to protect your account

To protect your eBay and PayPal accounts is really quite simple:

- Change your passwords regularly;

- Never reveal your password to anyone;

- Check your accounts regularly for any suspicious activity;

- Don't click on any 'Sign in' links in e-mails.

Columbia County Library
220 E. Main St.
P.O. Box 668
Magnolia, AR 71754-0668

Fake e-mails

From the day you open your account with either eBay or PayPal, you may be targeted by both amateur and highly professional crooks. They are hoping you will fall for their scams and fake e-mails and reveal your passwords and bank details, thus allowing them to steal from you and use your identity for bigger frauds.

Security tip

If there is one thing you remember from this book, then please let it be this: never reply to any e-mail asking you for your eBay or PayPal user ID, passwords or bank details, even if it looks like it is from eBay or PayPal.

Some fake e-mails are very easy to spot as they are written in very poor English, but the majority are convincing and well presented, copying eBay's logo and layout and showing the sender ID as eBay or PayPal.

All these fake e-mails have one thing in common: they ask for your password or bank details. To encourage you to reveal this, most e-mails will request you verify your account details as a matter of urgency to prevent your account being restricted or closed. Some will ask you to click on a link; this link takes you to a fake 'Sign on' page identical to eBay's own. The fraudsters use this fake page to capture your details.

If you receive any e-mail asking for confidential information, do not reply to it. You can report it via e-mail to spoof@ebay.co.uk for the UK or spoof@ebay.com for the US.

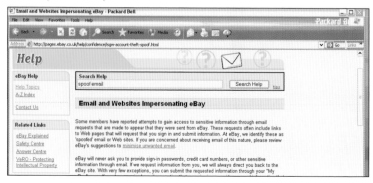

Another security measure is always to go direct to the eBay and PayPal pages. I would recommend you always open a new web browser when you access either site and type **www.ebay.co.uk** for the UK or **www.ebay.com** for the US. For PayPal use **www.paypal.com** when you wish to sign in to your account.

Security tip
Log in to your accounts regularly to check for any suspicious activity.

Imaginary items

As an eBay member, you may occasionally come across items for sale that don't exist. For example, I found the latest plasma television with a starting bid of 99p. I placed the item within my watch list and waited to place a bid towards the end of the auction. However, when I read the description carefully, I realised that I would have been bidding on an e-mail that will be sent to the highest bidder explaining where one could purchase the item at a 50% discount. I have never actually heard of anyone who has purchased items this way or who has saved money doing so. It is always a con trick to attract lots of people to part with a small amount of cash each.

There are many spins to this con trick. Some say you will receive a call giving you the information, others a voucher or a link to a special website where the goods are on sale. They all lead to nothing. My advice is to stay clear of them and look for genuine bargains.

eBay secrets tip
Always read item descriptions carefully before you bid, so you know exactly what you are bidding for.

Always tell yourself you don't get anything for nothing. I was on holiday in Spain with my family when I was approached by some scruffy guy asking me to try my luck on a free scratch card. Despite my refusal, he insisted on plunging this card in my hand and scratching the silver box for me.

What followed was a performance worth the highest acting award; it was clear he was in the wrong profession! He could not believe that I had won the jackpot prize of €1,000. He wanted to call a taxi right away for us to go and claim our prize in a new villa development outside the resort. I said, 'I'm not worthy of such a prize. You have been standing on a street corner all day in the heat of the sun, so you deserve it more than me.' He was quite taken aback when I said this; clearly this response was not in his well-rehearsed script! After a short time, while still walking with us, he explained that he was staff so he could not claim the prize. I insisted he took the ticket back and told him to give it a friend and split the money. With that he was gone. This €1,000 would have been a voucher towards a holiday that would have been at least €1,000 over-priced, and I would have had to sit through at least four hours of hard timeshare selling, as well as having to pay for my own taxi back.

When you come across a tempting bargain, don't forget to be cautious.

The long fraud

This is one of the most effective types of fraud found on eBay. A seller opens an eBay account and waits for, say, a year, building up positive feedback by purchasing small-value items from genuine sellers or selling the items to him or herself, using a different user ID. This is called shill bidding and is against eBay rules.

Then, all of a sudden, the seller will offer a high-value item such as a plasma or LCD television for sale. The seller might also ask to be paid using a money order. As you have probably guessed, the item never arrives.

Security tip
My advice is never to trade with buyers or sellers who ask for money orders. Also – and especially if you are buying any high-priced item – take some time to check out the seller's history and credentials before you make a bid.

Postage scam

Many eBay sellers will put a little extra on the true cost of postage and packing. This is very common as it gives sellers something for their time in packing up the parcel and taking it to the post office, and covers their seller's fees if the item sells at a very low price.

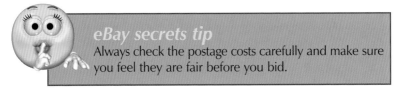

eBay secrets tip
Always check the postage costs carefully and make sure you feel they are fair before you bid.

However, there are some sellers who will make more on postage than they do for selling the item itself!

Another spin to this scam is for the seller to make a starting bid as postage. For example, I was looking for a notebook computer on eBay and found one that was new and had just 30 minutes left to run, with a bid of only £55.00. I thought it strange, so I looked carefully at the description.

The seller was charging £700 postage and packing, thus avoiding paying eBay's full fees on this expensive item. This might not seem a bad idea, but the problem occurs when things go wrong and you enter into a dispute with the seller. Instead of a dispute involving a £755 notebook computer, in the eyes of eBay it becomes a £55 notebook computer.

As well as checking postage costs carefully, you should also make sure that the seller is not going to add VAT to the cost of the item, as some VAT-registered users will try this. It's usually written somewhere in the item description. If a seller ever tries to add VAT later, refuse it.

Protection against viruses

Once you connect to the internet, your computer is at risk from viruses. These programs are designed to corrupt data and cause your computer to fail in one way or another.

Sophisticated spyware programs are also being used by criminals to gain access to your passwords and account information. Programmed to hunt out this information and to monitor keystrokes looking for unusual combinations of letters and numbers, they send such information back to the criminals within a fraction of a second. This is all done without your knowledge and with no symptoms appearing on your computer.

The only way to try to protect your computer is to install one of the many virus protection and spyware programs available and keep it up to date. Most programs offer an online update service. Also check with your internet service provider to see what help it offers. You should always back up valuable documents on CD or on a USB memory stick.

Security tip
Once you have installed virus protection and spyware on your PC, link to the live update every week to download the latest protection.

CHAPTER 4

Buying on eBay

In this chapter

- The bidding sequence
- The path to success
- The winner's curse
- What not to buy
- Who not to buy from
- Checking feedback
- Choosing your item
- Know the seller
- The reserve price
- Checking postage and packing
- Watching items
- Bid history
- Comparing auctions
- Buy it now
- Best offer
- When to make a bid
- Sniping for beginners
- How to make a bid
- Bid confirmation
- Checking your bid throughout the auction
- Bidding increments
- Bid retraction
- Item not won

Now you understand the basics, you are probably itching to get going and buy something on eBay. If you just take a little time to run through this chapter, then you will find it easier and you are more likely to guarantee a successful outcome – so be patient just a little longer.

The bidding sequence

You will understand the information in this chapter better if you know the basic sequence given below, but it is best to read through the whole chapter before you proceed.

- Sign in to your eBay account.

- Search for items you want using the search engine.

- Click on the item to take you to the product page.

- When you are sure you want to place a bid, click on **Place a bid**.

- Fill in the maximum amount you want to bid for the item and click on **Continue**.

- Check the details shown on the next screen and click on **Confirm bid**.

- If you are the highest bidder, this will be confirmed. If not, you can raise your maximum bid.

- You will receive an e-mail confirmation and the item will be listed in 'My eBay' under 'Items I'm bidding on'.

- If someone outbids you, you will receive an e-mail to let you know and encourage you to bid again. The item in 'My eBay' will appear in red instead of green.

The path to success

There are a few simple keys to successful buying on eBay.

- **Research the item:** Take your time to read the description carefully and make sure it is what you want. Look at the picture, check the specification and read the small print.

- **Check anything you are not sure about:** You can send an e-mail to the seller via the product page (see page 74).

- **Research the seller:** Check the seller's feedback to make sure he or she is a reliable source (see page 71).

Understand that popular items such as plasma/LCD televisions, MP3 players and computer games will attract lots of interest, as these products are in always in demand. Therefore you are unlikely to make huge savings when purchasing these. The real bargains are on the unusual and specialist items. If you are lucky and have followed my search advice you might have found items that are listed incorrectly or misspelt. These attract less interest and give you an opportunity to purchase a real bargain.

Buying on eBay flowchart

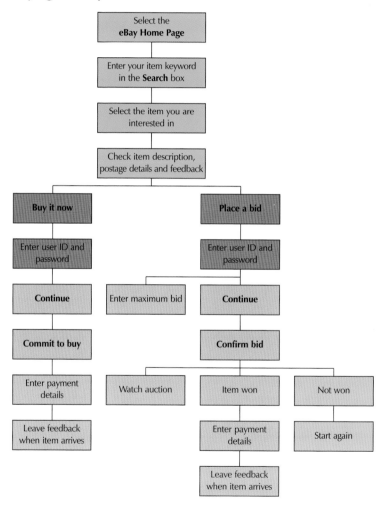

The winner's curse

'It's only worth what someone is willing to pay' is a cliché my father was fond of. When a seller lists an item on eBay it is offered to millions of potential buyers. It would be fair to say that the final price the item achieves in most cases reflects the market price. Therefore if you are the highest bidder and have outbid everyone else, you have paid more than what your rivals considered the item was worth. The more rivals watching and bidding, the less chance your item was a real bargain. This line of thought is generally forgotten, especially in the excitement felt during the closing few seconds of an auction. Before you start to bid, think about the 'winner's curse' that really states that the act of wining rules out getting a bargain because you have paid more than someone else was willing to pay.

What not to buy

Amongst the many millions of items for sale on eBay, a number of items are prohibited. Although eBay does its best to prevent many of these items from being listed, some will always get through. If you do attempt to purchase any such items, you do so at your own risk as prohibited items fall outside any buyer protection offered by eBay or PayPal. A full list can be found in eBay's 'Help' section under 'Prohibited, questionable and infringing items'.

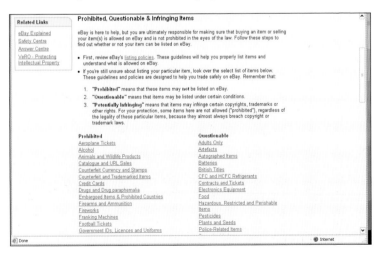

Who not to buy from

Most sellers on eBay are honest and reputable, but as in anything, there are a few bad apples and you need to be able to spot them. You can do this using eBay's feedback system (see page 71).

This is similar to the comments or visitors' book you might find in a hotel, but in an electronic form. Following a sale or purchase, both parties are invited to leave comments. These comments are listed on a members' site and can been seen by all eBay members.

Always check the feedback score of the seller. Look at the positive feedback and when the person became a member. In general, I would trust someone who has lots of positive feedback and who has been a member for over a year. As an added protection, never send money orders or cash. Instead, use PayPal and your credit card, especially for larger items.

If you do purchase something that has been incorrectly described in an attempt to attract bids, don't pay for it but contact the seller. If you have all ready paid, insist on a refund.

Security tip

Do your research. If a seller suddenly switches from selling cheap items to expensive luxury goods, alarm bells should ring.

A salutary lesson

No matter how careful you are you are, trust is still at the heart of eBay. I once placed a bid on a Lotus Elan sports car, described as 'in very good condition, low mileage'. I called the seller, asked some questions and was assured of the service history and what a great buy this car was. I won the car and, following the end of the auction, the seller insisted I send him a deposit. I refused and arranged to collect the car two days later.

We arrived early, hoping to catch the seller doing any last-minute repairs or trying to warm up the engine, and to give us time to look around the car. We found it was very tatty, with ripped seats and everything looking so worn out; you could easily see that it had accident damage that had been badly repaired. It was a death trap. The use of cable ties to hold parts of the cooling system did not impress me. The seller turned up, his hands covered in oil, 'Ready for a test drive?' he asked. 'No thanks, I'd rather see my children grow up,' I replied. I made it clear that I was not going to buy this car or even make him an offer. He tried to explain that the interior of the car belonged to a much older car, and was replaced. The wisdom of taking out the whole interior of a low-mileage car and replacing it with a very tatty ripped and smelly one did not make much sense to me.

I asked him strongly not to leave me negative feedback. 'You were bidding to buy not to view,' he complained (you will see this many times in the descriptions). I agreed, but the car was totally different from the description on eBay. Glad that I paid no deposit, I explained that my brother and I had taken time off work to collect this heap and travelled over 300 miles, so if anyone should be angry it should be us.

There are many bargains to be found on eBay, but if an item is too cheap you must spend time checking it out. Check the feedback left by buyers and look at the items and the price it achieved. If a seller gained a feedback score of 50, 100% positive but for items costing 99p, then suddenly started to sell Rolex watches at half price, I would think very carefully before placing a bid and parting with money. This type of fraud using the feedback system is known as the long fraud (see page 62).

Checking feedback

It is easy to check a member's feedback. Simply click on the user ID shown within the seller information box found on the auction page.

You have just selected this member's profile.

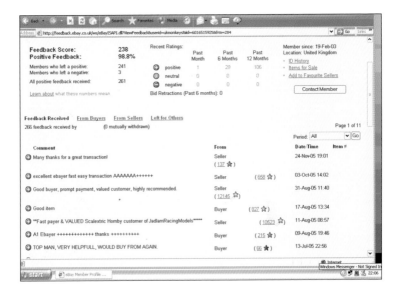

Now study the following:

- **Feedback Score:** The feedback score represents the number of eBay members that are satisfied doing business with a particular member. It is usually the difference between the number of members who left a positive rating and the number of members who left a negative rating

- **Positive Feedback:** This represents positive ratings left by members as a percentage.

- **Members who left positive:** This represents the number of members who have left a positive rating.

- **Members who left negative:** This represents the number of members who have left a negative rating.

- **All positive feedback received:** This represents the total number of instances of positive feedback received for all transactions, including repeat customers.

- **Recent ratings:** This table shows all of the ratings left for this member during the past month, six months and twelve months.

- **Bid retractions:** This shows the number of times a bid has been retracted (see page 88).

In an ideal world you should buy from a member who has a high feedback score together with high positive feedback. Click on some of the transactions to see if they are for small amounts or large amounts, and read the feedback left. If you have any doubts, don't buy from them. With the many millions of items appearing on eBay, it won't be long before it appears again, this time offered by a seller you can trust.

eBay secrets tip
Take the trouble to check a member's feedback. It could well stop you wasting your time and money.

Choosing your item

Once you have found the item you are interested in, you need to consider the following:

- Do I really want this?

- What's the cheapest price new in the shops?

- Is the item new or used; if used, how used?

- Is there any warranty?

- Have you read all of the item description?

- Is the description accurate or vague?

- Does the picture match the item or is it a sample?

- How much is postage?

- Is the feedback good?

Know the seller

If you are going to bid on expensive items, try to get to know your seller by asking questions about the item. You can learn a lot from the replies and the speed of the response.

The questions you should ask

You should always ask the seller questions about the item you are about to bid on. Start by asking questions that will confirm the condition and elicit any information you would like that is missing from the item description. Be specific. If you don't get a reply, this could mean that there is a problem with the item or the seller, so I would not proceed any further.

How to ask a question

• Access the auction page of the item you are interested in.

• Then select the **Ask seller a question** link found within the seller information box.

• Click on the type of question you wish to ask from the drop-down menu.

- Next type in your question and select the **Submit question** link. Before your question is sent you may be asked to copy the characters from a random text box into the blank box. This is to prevent automated questions being sent to eBay members.

- If the seller answers your question, then a copy of the reply is sent to your e-mail address.

eBay secrets tip

Don't be afraid to ask questions of the seller. If the answers aren't forthcoming, or if you're not happy with the replies, you could save yourself an expensive mistake.

The reserve price

Just like a non-internet auction, eBay offers its sellers the opportunity to set a reserve price. Buyers do not know the reserve price until bidding has exceeded it. Then a 'Reserve met' message is displayed within the listing. eBay sets a £50 minimum starting reserve, so all reserves are for £50 or higher on all listings.

Checking postage and packing

Before placing a bid, check the cost of postage and packing, and whether the seller will post the item to you. Most sellers will act honestly but some try and increase their profits by charging a much higher cost than you should be paying. If this happens to you, ask the seller, 'Why so high?' The chances are you won't get a reply, in which case I would not proceed with placing a bid.

Watching items

With all the items ending at different times you might think you will need to write them down. With your very own 'Watch list' you don't have to.

• From an auction page of the item you are interested in, select the **Watch this item** link found at the top right of the page.

• Once you have selected 'Watch this item' it is saved to your eBay page.

• To view your 'Watch list', select **My eBay** and all the items are displayed within the summary.

• If you wish to remove items from your 'Watch list' simply click the box next to the item, which places a tick within the box.

• Then select **Delete** and the item is removed.

Your watch list on eBay

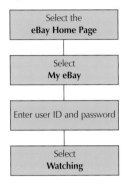

Select the
eBay Home Page

Select
My eBay

Enter user ID and password

Select
Watching

Bid history

As you watch an auction it's worthwhile keeping an eye on the bid history.

• From an auction page, select **Bids**.

• This page shows you the full history.

As you become more experienced, you will be able to gain lots of information from this, including:

• Number of bids;

• Number of bidders;

• Type of bidders and their habits;

• Level of interest.

Comparing auctions

When searching for an item, it's likely you will be presented with a number of auctions displaying your request. You could make a note of each one, but there is an easier way.

From your search results page, just click on the small box next to the item you wish to compare.

• Now click on another item you wish to compare. When finished, just click on the **Compare** link.

• You will then see the items displayed together.

Now you also have the option to add them to your 'Watch list' by clicking the **Watch all** link at the top of the page. The 'Compare' function will also work on all items within your watch list.

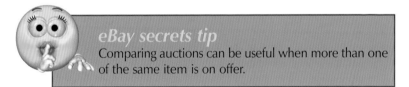

eBay secrets tip

Comparing auctions can be useful when more than one of the same item is on offer.

Buy it now

From time to time you will come across a listing with a 'Buy it now' option. This allows you to purchase the item instantly without the need to bid or wait until the auction finishes. There are two types: a fixed 'Buy it now', just like a price displayed in a shop is the price you pay; and an auction with a 'Buy it now' in which you are invited to bid for the item but have the option to end the auction early and purchase it at the 'Buy it now' price.

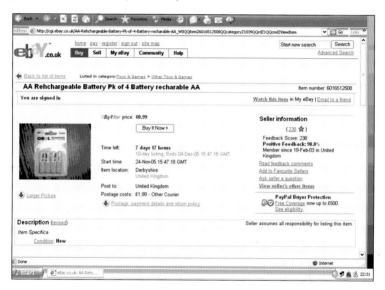

Best offer

New to eBay is an option called 'Best offer' located next to the 'Buy it now' option on the listing. If you see 'Submit your best offer', then you select this link to make the seller an offer. Both buyers and sellers should understand that this forms the binding terms of an agreement, if accepted. Once your offer has been sent, you may track the progress within 'My eBay'. The seller has 48 hours to think about your offer.

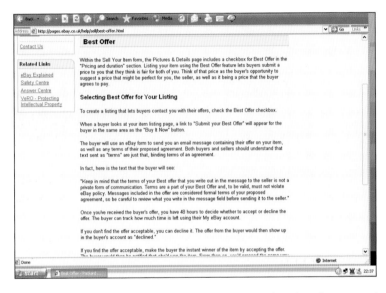

If the seller turns down your offer the word 'Declined' will appear. If your offer is accepted then you will be sent the 'Winner' e-mail and you must complete the sale in the normal way.

When to make a bid

Resist the temptation to rush in and bid, unless there are only a few seconds left before the auction ends. Add the item to your 'Watch list' so it can be found again quickly and easily within 'My eBay'.

You may place a bid any time before the auction ends. The best time to make a bid is during the closing few seconds of the auction. This is known as sniping. If you can't be at your computer during the closing few minutes of the auction – and remember you can use any computer, it does not have to be your own – then you must make your bid as late as possible.

Sniping for beginners

There are many bidding strategies, all claiming to improve your chances of winning the auction. Most experienced eBayers understand how the bidding system works and will formulate their own system, which I'm sure in time you will do. For now I will tell you one of mine:

• First decide your maximum bid, taking into account the condition of the item and the postage cost. Stick to this price and never increase it.

• Place two maximum bids, one during the last two minutes and the other during the last 30 seconds or less, depending on the speed of your internet connection.

• Bid a round amount first followed by one with a few more pence added. This is because most eBay members bid in round numbers. For example, let's say the maximum you wish to bid is £10 and a few pence. First place a maximum bid of £7 two minutes before the auction ends. Now place another maximum bid of £10.67 regardless of whether you are winning or not. The eBay system will always take the higher amount, should another member start to bid against you.

How to make a bid

All being well, you will have done all your research, you have a maximum bid in your head and you are now ready to bid.

- Open the auction page you are interested in and click on the **Place a bid** link

- Enter your maximum bid. Remember: if you are sniping this should be the first of your two maximum bids. If you can't be there to watch the end of the auction, place your maximum bid now and click **Continue**.

- You are about to make a bid that is legally binding. Check all the details, including your maximum bid, and only when you are happy should you click on **Submit**.

Bid confirmation

• If you have been successful, the message 'You are the current high bidder' is displayed.

• If your bid was unsuccessful, the message 'You have been outbid by another bidder' is displayed. You will then be invited to bid again.

Checking your bid throughout the auction

It's important to check your bid status often, especially in the closing few seconds. During an auction if you have been outbid, an e-mail will be sent to you, but this is not as quick as if you check your own bid status. You can do this as follows:

• First open the auction page you are interested in.

• Click on the **Refresh** button within your browser. This updates the page including the time remaining and bid information.

• During the closing few seconds of an auction you may find yourself refreshing the page many times. For many members, this is the most exciting part of eBay.

• If you have been outbid, you may place another bid anytime before the auction ends.

Bidding increments

Bidding increments are set by eBay. Values at the time of going to press are given in Appendix II (see page 138).

eBay secrets tip
Don't get caught up in a bidding frenzy. In the heat of the moment you might find yourself bidding – and paying – well above your planned maximum bid.

Bid retraction

It is possible for you to retract your bid, but by bidding you have committed yourself to a legal contract. There are only a few circumstances in which you may retract a bid:

• You clearly entered the wrong bid amount – for example, £1,000 instead of £10.00;

• You can't contact the seller;

• The description does not match the item.

This is how you retract a bid:

- Open the auction page you have placed a bid on, then make a note of the item number. You will need this later.

- Next select the **Bid history** link.

- Located at the bottom of the 'Bid history' page, click on **Retract your bid**.

• You must now read the 'Bid retraction' form. If you are happy, continue by selecting the Bid retraction form link at the bottom of the page.

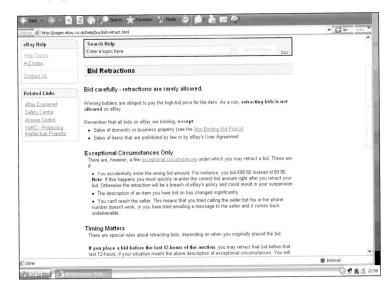

• Enter the item number and select a reason for your bid retraction from the drop-down list. Finally, click **Retract bid**.

It is very important you don't do this too many times because bid retractions are recorded and can be seen by all eBay members. As an alternative, you can ask the seller to cancel your bid.

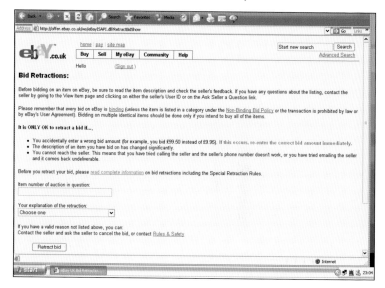

Item not won

If you have been outbid and have not won your item, don't worry. Any fool can win an auction by simply paying much more than the item is worth! Remember: there are new items appearing on eBay all the time so be patient and I'm sure you will have another opportunity to bid.

CHAPTER 5

You're a Winner

In this chapter

- ⊛ How to pay
- ⊛ Leaving feedback
- ⊛ Item does not arrive
- ⊛ Damaged and poorly described items
- ⊛ Seller disputes

If you are the highest bidder when the auction finishes, congratulations: you're a winner. A message 'The item is yours' will appear within the auction page and an e-mail will be sent to you.

How to pay

Below the congratulations message on the auction page you will find a 'Pay now' button and the methods of payment accepted by the seller. You will also find this button and payment information within an e-mail that will be sent.

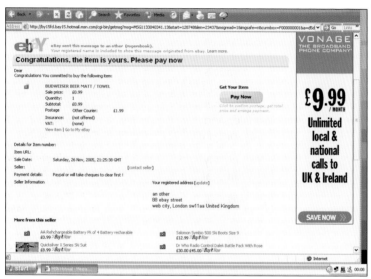

Remember that all items that are won and that you are watching or bidding on can be found within 'My eBay'.

Select the **Pay now** button and choose your method of payment from the options preferred by the seller. Once you have completed this, you can check the status within 'My eBay'. If you are sending a cheque or cash, don't forget to include a copy of the auction page with your name and address. If you have no printer, write down the item number with a description and your name and address.

Leaving feedback

By now you should have a good understanding of the feedback system and appreciate that it is at the heart of eBay. It's what's used to judge other eBay members. Positive feedback helps members sell their goods, whereas negative feedback warns off buyers. Before you ever leave negative feedback, you must work with the seller or buyer to resolve any problems. Only when you can't resolve problems should you leave negative feedback. As well as positive/negative feedback there is neutral feedback, but this isn't used very often because many eBay members regard it just the same as negative feedback. I would use neutral feedback if the seller were difficult to deal with or slow to help if there were problems with the item, but if after much time, trouble, and persistence – rather than the seller wishing to help – it was sorted out and I was happy with the item.

To leave feedback, click on **My eBay link** followed by the **Feedback** link located within **My summary**.

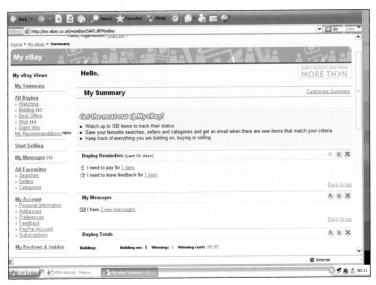

Now simply click on the **Leave feedback** link next to the relevant item.

Nine times out of ten you will click the 'Positive' feedback button. Then leave you comments – for instance, good to deal with, quick purchase, excellent. Remember to check the feedback you leave before selecting **Leave feedback**. Once left, it's virtually impossible to change.

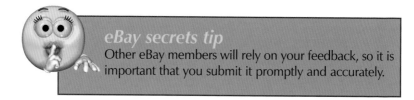

eBay secrets tip

Other eBay members will rely on your feedback, so it is important that you submit it promptly and accurately.

Item does not arrive

If after a while your item does not arrive, first contact the seller and ask for confirmation of when the item was sent. The seller might have simply forgotten to post it. Be friendly as the problem could be with the courier and not the seller. Always try your best to work problems out with the seller, but if you are making no progress then contact eBay. You can report your problem and the seller to eBay through the 'Help' link. eBay will then begin investigating and all being well resolve your problems.

Damaged and poorly described items

Always contact the seller first in a timely manner. The quicker you report problems to the seller the better, because there may only be a limited time to make a claim with the courier. It is vital to keep all communications friendly and polite.

I once received a damaged toy. I suspected the seller knew this because he said he had 'never tried' the part that was damaged. The damage halved the value. The seller agreed and offered a 50% refund if I wished to keep the item. I accepted, as it was a bargain to begin with. Only after you have tried your best should you report the seller to eBay and start proceedings to recover your money for damaged or badly described items.

eBay secrets tip

Don't hesitate to report an unhelpful seller to eBay. You can do this via the 'Help' section under 'Dispute resolution'.

Seller disputes

If you have followed my advice and researched both the item and the seller, then disputes should be rare. However, there are some bad apples, and eBay has established a system for minimising their impact and looking into problems. If you have tried your best to communicate with the seller without success, you should report them to eBay. Select **Help** and then search **Dispute resolution** and follow the instructions you find there.

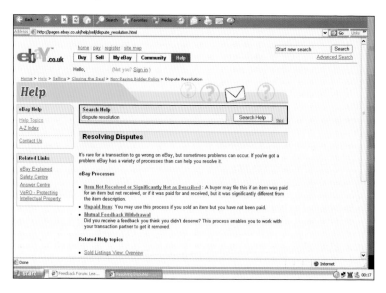

CHAPTER 6

Ready to Sell

Successful selling

Just about anything will sell on eBay if the price is right, even a bit of old rope! I'm sure you've heard lots of stories of how thousands of people are making lots of money using eBay. But there is only one way of making money on eBay and that is to sell items for more than you paid for them. This is simple advice that is often forgotten within all the hype surrounding eBay and the many books on the subject.

I knew someone who bought items on eBay and then relisted them back on eBay hoping to make a profit. It never worked. I knew another person who would list items that were on sale from a discount wholesale warehouse. He relied on making a small profit on a high volume. He enjoyed limited success. eBay can be the place to buy from if you have a retail shop where most of your customers won't have access to eBay and therefore its bargains. Most eBay members make money from buying items from car boots, garage sales, flea markets, house clearances and free ad papers and then cleaning them up before finally listing them on eBay. If you have your own business or hobby that involves making something others might want then eBay could be the place for you to show off your products and make some money. Other older eBay members sell unwanted jewellery, antiques and collectables acquired over many years, giving them extra money in their retirement.

Whatever you are going to sell, follow the advice within this chapter and you will achieve the best price for your item.

Check your auction on eBay flowchart

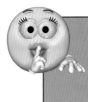

eBay secrets tip
Never lose sight of the fact that the only way to make money on eBay is to sell items for more than you paid for them.

What to sell and what not to sell

Just about anything sells on eBay. If the price is right, there are always going to be items that appeal to many eBay members – for example, the latest flat-screen television, mobile phone, video game or MP3 player. If you want to know the latest must-haves and popular items that members are searching for, select the eBay pulse link from eBay's home page.

There are a number of prohibited items that you are not allowed to sell under eBay rules and polices. These include firearms, drugs, fireworks, credit cards and body parts. A full list of prohibited items, together with an explanation, can be found in eBay's 'Help' section under 'Prohibited, questionable and infringing items'.

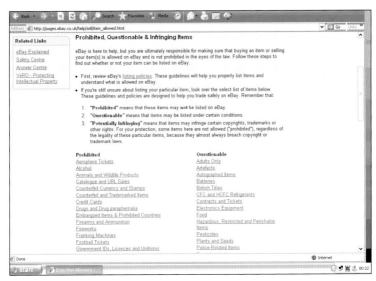

What it's worth

I will remind you of what my father said to me: 'It's only worth what someone else is willing to pay.' First search eBay for an item identical to the one you are thinking about selling. Add the results to your 'Watch list' so you can track bids through 'My eBay'. You now have to wait for the auction to finish. Remember that most bidding occurs during the closing few minutes, so don't judge the value of your item before the auction ends. Also consider that eBay might not be the best place to sell your item. If it's a specialist piece worth a lot of money, then there are specialist sales that will attract buyers who have a particular interest in your item. If you have a high value item you wish to sell, always seek a professional valuation.

The starting price

There are really two main lines of thought regarding the starting price:

• The starting price should be really low so as to attract as much interest and bids as possible;

• The starting price should be the lowest price you are prepared to let the item go for.

Both lines of thought are right, although I would always start by thinking of the lowest price you're prepared to accept after considering what the item cost. With this figure in mind I would take a little money off to make it attractive. If it sells for the starting bid then just tell yourself that was what the item was worth and you will make up any loss you feel you have made on the next item you sell.

The reserve price

Just like a real auction, you may set a reserve price for your item. However, a reserve is likely to put some eBay members off bidding. I would always favour using a starting bid as your reserve if you really want to guarantee the money you will receive.

eBay secrets tips

eBay sets a £50 minimum starting reserve, so all reserves are for £50 or higher on all listings.

Buy it now

You might not be able to list a 'Buy it now' price at first (see page 81) as eBay insists you have a feedback score of 10. With experience you will learn when to use this feature but for now we will put it to one side.

Best offer

New to eBay is an option called 'Best Offer' (see page 82). Bidders are invited to make you an offer on your listed item. Once an offer has been sent you may accept or reject it.

Timing your auction

An auction may last up to ten days. In theory the longer the time you list your item, the more eBay members will have the opportunity to view your listing. However, there may be times when you will have to list your item for a short duration. For example, you might want your auction to finish before someone else's, with a similar item finishes, especially if it's a specialist item that will only attract a couple of bidders.

When to start and finish your auction

There are so many theories and strategies regarding the timing of your auction. My general advice would be to have your auction finish on a Sunday evening at a time that does not clash with any major sporting events, popular television shows or popular holiday times. If this is not possible, try to time the ending of the auction to finish when the majority of people are at home, probably early evening. I've found that if you can wait until the end or start of the month, this too can have an effect on the price your item achieves.

Multiple items and Dutch auctions

These auctions are when a seller has identical items for sale. Rather than list each one individually, the seller may list them all in a single auction. The bidders are invited to specify the quantity they would like and the price they are willing to pay. In this auction, all the highest bidders pay the same price.

Select a category

As discussed earlier (see page 30), the category in which an item for sale is placed can influence how easy it is to find by potential buyers searching. You need to choose a category for listing your item for sale. Enter a keyword that matches your item in the search box within 'Sell your item' and eBay will suggest a category for the top level. Now keep moving from box to box making your selection, then click on the **Continue** link.

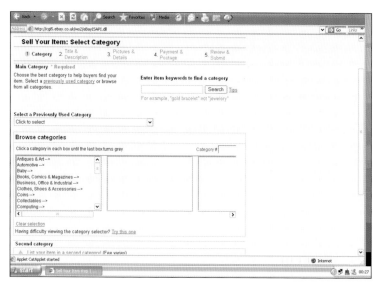

Choosing your title

A title should always contain the keywords used to find your item. If you are selling a Philips Plasma Television, then within the title should be 'Philips Plasma Television'. You might also want to include 'Brand New' if it's new and the screen size. Remember: eBay's search engine works on the words used with your description.

eBay secrets tip
If you fail to use the most appropriate keywords to describe your item, then eBay members won't be able to find it.

A picture paints a thousand words

Unlike a conventional shop, buyers can't examine or handle goods. Your customers have to rely on your description and, if possible, a photograph. I would not buy anything without seeing it first.

Pictures taken with a digital camera will greatly enhance your listing. The benefit of going digital is that it allows you to take and view your pictures in an instant. If you're not happy with the picture, you can delete it and take another. There is now a huge range of digital cameras on sale starting from around £20 to a few thousand pounds. You don't need anything fancy or to spend lots of money to get really good results.

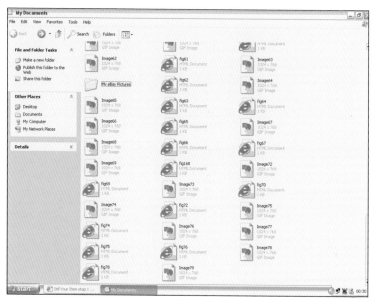

Most digital cameras are really easy to use. A reputable retailer will allow you to try them out in the shop for yourself. Check that the camera includes the software and USB lead needed to transfer your pictures from your camera to your computer. When you've found a camera you like, don't forget to search eBay for it and see if you can buy it cheaper!

Transferring pictures from your camera to your computer varies from camera to camera, so you will need to refer to the manual and quick start guide. You will need to be able to find your pictures quickly, so make sure you create a folder on your computer for them and give them a file name you will recognise.

Taking pictures

I'm no photographer, but I've achieved some excellent results. Here are my tips:

• Adjust the file size of your picture first within your camera settings. On some cameras this could be known as 'quality'. The higher the quality, the bigger the file size. Try setting the resolution setting to 640 x 480, which should reduce the file size. File size is important because it needs to be under 100KB for you to be able to upload the image to eBay quickly; the average is about 50KB.

• Take lots of pictures and try different angles.

• Turn off the flash if you are going to take pictures of items in blister packs or items with a shiny surface, as the reflection can often be seen.

• If you are selling an item that is damaged, it's wise to take a picture and show the damage. Hiding it will only cause you problems later.

• Always make sure the picture you use is in focus with nothing else going on in the background to distract the viewer.

eBay secrets tip
As an alternative to a digital camera, you could use a web cam. The quality won't be as good, but it is better than no picture at all.

Gallery options

I would always consider the first option, 'Gallery picture'. Selecting this will allow buyers to see a photo of your item next to your description on the search results page. This option will use the picture you set as photo 1. The second option, 'Gallery featured', should only be considered once you have gained some experience, because there is a higher cost involved.

You have a few more options, such as bold and highlighted, that can really make an impact, but for now if you are happy select **Continue**.

Sell locally or internationally

Listing your item with eBay allows you to attract many millions of potential buyers. Most of transactions will take place within your own country, but if you feel confident enough then you can offer your item internationally, attracting overseas interest (see page 33).

Payment methods

Before you list your item within your auction, carefully consider all your payment options again (see page 33) and their advantages and disadvantages. Remember: limiting your payment options might also limit the number of bidders.

eBay secrets tip
Make sure you research thoroughly your methods of payment, the postage costs and insurance.

Postage and packing

If you are sending a small item where the postage cost is only a few pence, you might want to offer your item 'post free'. This will make your auction more attractive. In most cases you will add a cost for postage and packing to your item. Always be honest and work out the cost of your packing material and postage. If you're going to add a bit extra, make sure it *is* only a bit. Remember: a high postage cost will be very off-putting to many eBay members.

Insurance

Many carriers will offer insurance at an extra cost. You might want to offer this option to your customers, together with Recorded or Special Delivery. If they turn down these options, remind them that postage is at their risk and you won't replace the item, should it get lost.

Customer care

Customer care is at the heart of all successful companies and should therefore be high on your list. Poor customer care will lead to negative feedback. It does not take much to give an excellent service to your customers. Here are a few top tips:

* Respond quickly to all requests and always be polite.

* Be truthful and helpful when you receive questions.

* Pack items with care.

* Post them as soon as payment is received.

Step-by-step guide to listing your item

* From the eBay home page select the **Sell** tab.

* Now click on **Sell your item**.

- For now we are only interested in **Sell at online auction**, so click on this option, if it's not already highlighted, and then **Continue**.

- Now select **Browse through categories**. Choose your first category and keep clicking on the boxes until finished. Don't worry about a second category for now. When you've finished, click **Continue**.

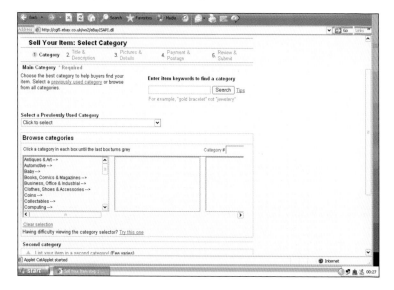

• Now complete the item title, remembering to use keywords.

• You now have the chance to include a subtitle, at an extra cost. This can be useful, but it really depends upon your item.

• Next is the 'Condition' tab. You may if you wish select **New** or **Used** or leave blank. You're now ready to move on to the all important **Item description**. Take your time and experiment with different fonts, sizes and colours to create a really attractive ad. When you've finished, click **Continue**.

• Choose your starting price and remember to be realistic.

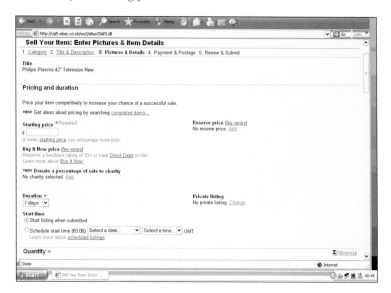

• Now choose your auction duration. If you don't wish your auction to start when your listing is submitted, you have the option to select a date and time for your auction to begin. eBay will make a small charge for this.

• Next is the 'Quantity' tab, for if you have more than one of the same item. This option might not be available to new members.

- Next is the option to add your pictures. Click the **Browse** button to select the location of your first photo, which should always be your best one. If you have more than one photo, select the other **Browse** button for your second photo.

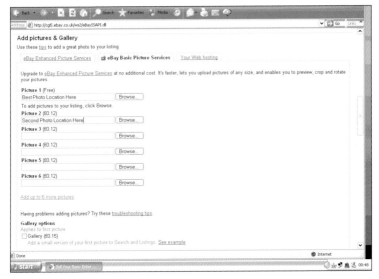

Payment and postage

Select and highlight the payment methods you are prepared to accept. If PayPal is one of your choices, check that your e-mail address is shown correctly.

Check and highlight the locations you are prepared to post to and then enter your postal cost for the item, remembering to add the cost of materials used for packing. You have a few more options, but again for now I would skip these and move to 'Payment instructions'. Give clear instructions on how and when you would like to be paid and your postage cost.

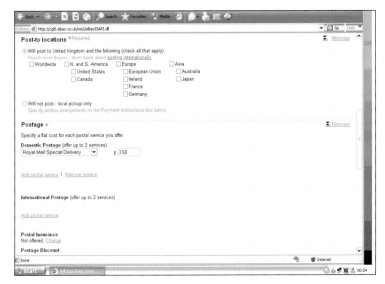

When you're happy, click **Continue**.

It's a very good idea now to check and review your listing.

Only when you are completely satisfied should you select the **Submit listing** button.

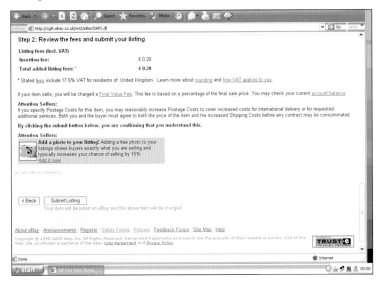

Revising your listing

You *can* revise your listing at anytime after you have submitted it, providing you have received no bids. However, this will show up on your listing as 'Revised', which might put off bidders. Once you have received a bid on your item, eBay will limit some of the revisions you are able to make.

Listing fees

There are a number of listing options to enhance your item listing. Those at the time of going to press are given in Appendix III (see page 139).

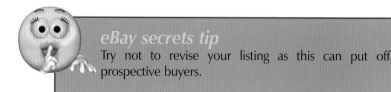

eBay secrets tip

Try not to revise your listing as this can put off prospective buyers.

CHAPTER 7

Your Item Has Sold

In this chapter

- ❂ Getting paid
- ❂ Unpaid items
- ❂ Posting your item
- ❂ Problems after postage
- ❂ Leaving feedback

Congratulations, if you are reading this following the sale of your item. eBay will automatically send you and your buyer a confirmation e-mail. Within your buyer's e-mail there is all he or she needs to complete the sale. There is not really much you need to do, as most eBay members will complete the process quickly. When the checkout process has been completed, it will be noted within 'My eBay' If your buyer has paid via PayPal, you will receive a 'You've got new funds' e-mail.

An e-mail will also be sent once your buyer has completed the checkout process. If payment is to be made by cheque or postal order, remember to wait and allow time for the payment to arrive and, in the case of a cheque, for it to clear, before sending your item.

Getting paid

Most eBay members will complete the checkout process quickly; eBay recommends that buyers and sellers should contact each other within three days of the auction ending. If your buyer has not completed the checkout process within this time you need to send a reminder. Go to **My eBay** and select the **Sold** link.

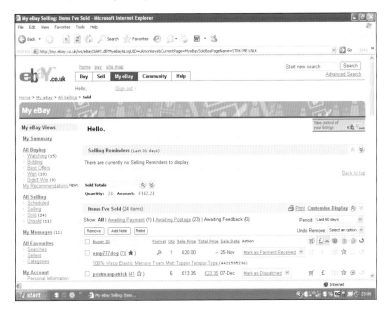

Now select the item you are waiting payment for and send a second invoice.

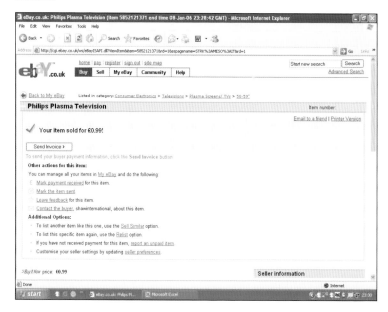

Previously, following the sale of your item, eBay would have sent you an e-mail with the contact details of your buyer. I would also use this information to send your buyer a polite e-mail enquiring if there is a problem – and it *is* important to be polite. Life would be boring if everyone was the same, so be patient and helpful.

eBay secrets tip

Give difficult buyers every opportunity to complete the sale before reporting them to eBay for non-payment.

Unpaid items

The majority of eBay members are honest, but if you are unlucky enough to encounter a buyer who refuses to pay and you have tried to contact them by being polite, then it's time to file an unpaid item dispute. You have up to 45 days following the end of your auction to do this, but I would wait no longer than two weeks. First log in to your eBay account then go to **My eBay** and check to see if any payment has been made by going to **Sold** and selecting the item you are waiting payment on. If no payment has been received, go to the **Unpaid item links** or select the **Help** tab and search **Unpaid items**. This will bring you to a link to report an unpaid item. The form you need to complete is simple; the only hard part is making sure you have the correct item number and this is always found next to your listed item.

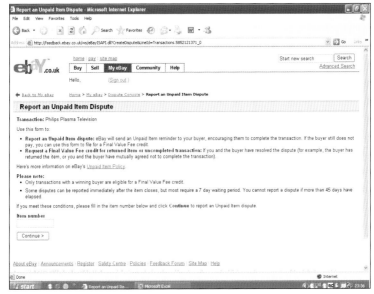

Once you file an unpaid item dispute, you can keep track of the progress within 'My eBay'. If your buyer still refuses to pay, then your final value fee is returned to you via eBay, this being the commission you pay eBay once your item has sold. Your buyer will receive a warning from eBay: a 'strike' for non-payment. If an eBay member receives three strikes then they are 'out' and their account is suspended, preventing them from trading on eBay.

Posting your item

Once you have received payment, it is best to post the item to your customer as soon as possible. I always send an e-mail thanking them for their custom and letting them know the item was sent. Remember: it's your responsibility to ensure the item reaches your buyer. I always send valuable items by registered post. A quick service will often result in positive feedback.

Problems after posting

It's rare to have problems after you have posted the item to your customer but if you do it's likely to be:

Item did not arrive

Assure your customer it was posted and, if you have it, send them proof of posting. Work with your customer to sort things out. If they did not take your offer of insurance up or to pay extra for the item to be sent recorded delivery, then remind your buyer of this. Be polite and remember it's your responsibility to ensure the item reaches the buyer in good condition. If you can claim for the loss of the item, do this as soon as possible.

Item arrives damaged

Providing you pack items well you should not encounter many claims as a result of damage. There are some items that just don't travel well, and I would always list such items as being for 'local pick-up only' Again, always be polite, even if it's not your fault. Ask your buyer to retain all the packing as this may be required by the courier, should you make a claim.

eBay secrets tip
Remember: it's up to you to sort out any problems, not the buyer.

Item not as described

If your customer is unhappy with the item you posted, you must listen carefully to what they have to say. It could be that your description of the item was incorrect or misleading. If this is the case then I would recommend you bend over backwards to resolve the problem to your buyer's complete satisfaction, even if it means you lose money. If it's a simple misunderstanding, negotiate with your buyer. Offer some money off. If your buyer insists on a refund, only refund the cost of the item and not the post and packing cost. Do this only when the item is safely in your hands and you have inspected it.

Leaving feedback

We have already discussed the importance of leaving feedback. It's really the same process as if you were leaving it for something you have purchased. Once you have received payment and your buyer has also safely received the item, it's a good idea to leave feedback. Go to **My eBay** and select the **Feedback** link. The process is the same as described on page 95). Remember to leave positive feedback, unless you had a really bad experience and negative feedback is justified.

CHAPTER 8

Your Item Has Not Sold

No bids? Don't worry

Don't worry if your item hasn't sold. There are many reasons why items don't attract any bids; here are my top four:

• Item too expensive;

• Poor use of keywords;

• Uninspiring or poor item description;

• Item not wanted at any price.

Take another look at your listing and consider if your item falls into any of the above.

Research more

Did you really research your item before listing it on eBay? If similar items are selling or attracting bids on eBay, clearly you are either unlucky or there is something about your listing that is deterring bidders. Look carefully at listings of items similar to yours that are attracting bids and if necessary copy their style, but do it in your own words. Make sure you copy their starting price, too!

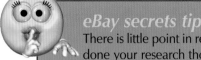

eBay secrets tip
There is little point in relisting your item unless you have done your research thoroughly.

Sell elsewhere

If there is no item like yours on eBay, it's either very rare and worth some money or its rubbish! You might be the only person in the world who thinks this item is worth paying money for. If you have a local second-hand shop or auction room, I would take your item there and ask for a valuation, and also how much they would be prepared to pay you now for it. If no one wants it, it's very likely no eBay members would want it either. Take it to a local charity shop where with a bit of luck they might be able to sell it. The feeling of doing some good would be a greater reward than any money you would get for your item.

Relist your item

Sometimes it's worth just trying again. If your item has not sold, select **My eBay** and then under 'All selling' select **Unsold**.

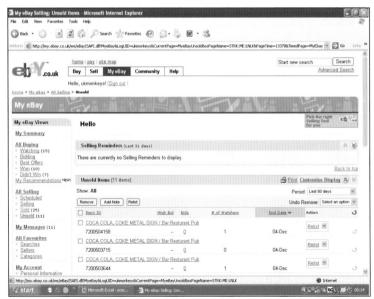

Now click on **Relist item** located next to your auction listing.

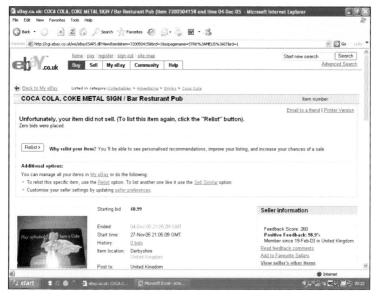

Your listing is now displayed, together with eBay's recommendations on making your item more appealing.

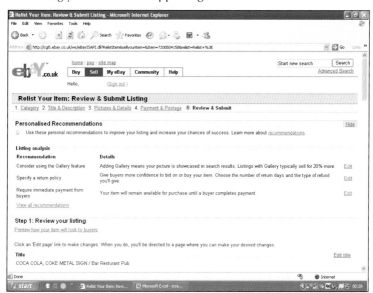

The eBay recommendations are only *recommendations*; they don't guarantee that you will sell your item, so think twice about taking them up. Use the information together with your own research to make the changes you feel are needed to make your item more attractive to eBay members.

Make your changes by selecting the **Edit** link next to the heading you would like to change. When you are happy with your listing, select **Submit listing**.

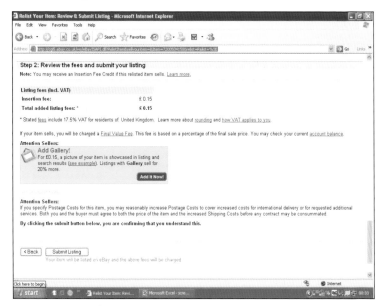

CHAPTER 9

Tips for Success

The aim of this book is to guide you through the registration process and help you buy and sell on eBay successfully, but there are many features within eBay we have not explored.

To add to the knowledge you have gained so far, here are a few of my own tips for success that I hope you will find useful. They are not advanced but do require you to have become familiar with the basic selling and buying concepts explained within this book. For your knowledge and experience to grow, you must use the eBay site and practise the skills you have gained from this book.

Buying tips

• **Check the level of interest.** Use the counter at the bottom of most auction listings to check the level of interest before placing a bid. An item with no bids but 7,000 page views means there will be a few eBay members watching this item waiting to place a bid at the last moment.

• **Use the system.** Save your favourite searches and activate eBay's notification service. It's great to receive an e-mail telling you that eBay has found an item for you. It also saves a lot of time.

• **Synchronise your clock.** Make sure the time on your clock is the same as eBay time.

- **Buy a countdown timer.** For last-second bidding (sniping) buy yourself a cheap digital kitchen countdown timer. Set it to five or ten minutes. When the item you are watching reaches the same remaining time, start your countdown timer. It's a simple and reliable way of judging when to make your last-second bid.

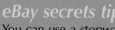

eBay secrets tip

You can use a stopwatch to time your last-second bid, but in the excitement it is easy to forget the time you are watching.

- **Make a 'Buy it now' offer.** New members are often unaware that many eBay members wait almost to the end of the auction before placing a bid. Contact the new member selling the item you are interested in through **Ask a question** and politely ask if you could make them a 'Buy it now' offer as you have noticed their item has attracted no bids. If the seller agrees, ask them to add 'Buy it now' to their listing at your agreed price.

- **Maintain your protection.** If the seller simply asks for payment then removes the auction listing, this is against eBay rules so you proceed at your own risk. You will not be covered by either eBay or PayPal buyer protection programmes.

- **Do your research.** Research carefully items you are buying. Call in to local stores and see similar items for yourself; sometimes they are not as good as you first thought.

- **Don't exceed your stated price.** Know your upper limit for bidding and don't exceed it.

- **Don't buy memorabilia.** Never buy autographs or memorabilia. Fakes are common on eBay and are hard to spot. I've known sellers use a photo of the original purchase receipt to sell hundreds of copies.

- **Collect in person.** Ask the seller if this is possible whenever you can. You will save on postage and packing, and will also have the opportunity to inspect your purchase.

Selling tips

- **Take pictures.** Take lots of pictures using your digital camera. The more pictures you take, the greater the chance that you will take a fantastic one.

- **Use the gallery option.** Always select the 'Gallery' option, as buyers like to see what they are buying.

- **Check your keywords.** Make sure you use keywords that match your item.

- **Time your start and finish.** Follow my earlier advice on when to start your auction listing (see page 103), but if there is an item already listed that is similar to yours, time your auction to end a little earlier, particularly if it's not such a popular item.

- **Keep an eye on progress.** When you have started your auction listing, keep track on the progress within 'My eBay'. Use the information to judge interest in your item.

eBay secrets tip

The number of people watching your item often become bidders, so keep an eye on progress via 'My eBay'.

- **Respond quickly.** Answer all members' questions quickly and use the opportunity to really sell your item in your reply.

- **Check feedback.** Check the feedback score of bidders and look at their history. If your item has attracted a poor payer or timewaster, then, depending on the value of what you are selling, say you would like a deposit or you will cancel their bid.

- **Post quickly.** Once you've received payment, post your item to the buyer as soon as possible.

Glossary

Advanced search: In-depth search for specific items.

Bidder: An eBay member who takes part in an auction.

Bid increments: Amounts by which bids are increased.

Bid retraction: Withdrawal of a bid by a buyer.

Buy it now: Allows members to purchase the item at a fixed price.

Category: Classification system used by eBay for items on sale.

Chargeback: Claim for the return of payment made through PayPal or through your credit card company.

Dutch auction: Auction that allows multiple items to be offered. All winners pay the same price.

Feedback: eBay system that allows members to judge one another, following transactions, expressed as a percentage.

Fixed price: *see* Buy it now

Gallery: Listing enhancement for your pictures.

Highest bidder: eBay member with the highest bid in an auction.

Insertion fees: *see* Listing fees

Listing: Auction or 'Buy it now' advert on eBay.

Listing fees: Charges made by eBay for putting an item for sale.

Maximum bid: Highest price you are willing to bid. eBay will bid for you up to this price.

Member profile: File of details about an eBay member.

My eBay: Space on eBay showing all your eBay account details and activities.

NARU: Not a registered user. Used when a member has been banned as a result of rule breaking.

Registered user: eBay member.

Reserve price: Minimum price a seller sets for their item.

Scheduled listing: Date and time you chose for your item to be listed.

Shill bidding: Setting up of another account to bid against yourself to increase the price and interest in your item. Friends of the seller may also be asked to bid. Shill bidding is against eBay rules.

Sniping: Placing a last-second bid moments before the auction ends.

Spoof e-mails: E-mail requests sent by criminals asking you to reveal your account details.

Starting price: Lowest price the seller will accept as an opening bid.

Subtitle: Listing enhancement extra to the listing title.

Watch list: List of items you are interested in, which can be viewed in 'My eBay'.

Bidding increments

Values at January 2006

Bid amount low	Bid amount high	Bid increment
£0.01	£1.00	£0.05
£1.01	£5.00	£0.20
£5.01	£15.00	£0.50
£15.01	£60.00	£1.00
£60.01	£150.00	£2.00
£150.01	£300.00	£5.00
£300.01	£600.00	£10.00
£600.01	£1,500	£20.00
£1,500.01	£3,000	£50.00
£3,000.01	And above	£100.00

Basic insertion fees and final value fees

Insertion Fees — Values at January 2006

Starting or reserve price	Insertion fee
£0.01–£0.99	£0.15
£1.00–£4.99	£0.20
£5.00–£14.99	£0.35
£15.00–£29.99	£0.75
£30.00–£99.99	£1.50
Upwards	£2.00

Final Value Fees — Values at January 2006

Closing price	Final value fee
Item not sold	No fee
£0.01–£29.99	5.25% for the amount of the high bid (at the listing close for auction-style listings) up to £29.99
£30.00–£599.99	5.25% of the initial £29.99 (£1.57), plus 3.25% of the remaining closing value balance
Over £600.00	5.25% of the initial £29.99 (£1.57), plus 3.25% of the initial £30.00 – £599.99 (£18.53), plus 1.75% of the remaining closing value balance

The insertion fee for multiple item (Dutch) auctions and fixed price listings is based upon the opening value of your items. The opening value is the starting price or the fixed price multiplied by the quantity of your items. The maximum insertion fee for any multiple item listing is £3.00.

The final value fee for a multiple item (Dutch) auction is determined by taking the final value fee of the lowest successful bid and multiplying it by the number of items sold. Multiple item, fixed price listing is calculated per item sold, based on the final sale price of the item.

Index